BAR TRICKS

This outrageous new handbook includes...

SIMPLE STRAW FUN—How to use ordinary drinking straws, toothpicks or matchsticks in games of chance ... and mind-bending puzzles.

BOTTLE BLOW AWAYS—Simple tricks with glass bottles that stagger the imagination.

GLASS GASSERS—Side-splitting dares that dazzle your friends with ordinary soda glasses, beer mugs or shot glasses.

DOLLAR BILL BETS—How to fool your friends with deceptively simple dollar bill games.

COIN CORKERS—A penny for your thoughts ... and a quarter for a load of laughs.

MIND BLOWERS—Wild and weird little tricks that strain the brain.

FUN! SIMPLE! STEP-BY-STEP!

D0564285

BAR TRICKS

THOMAS E. KILLEN

BERKLEY BOOKS, NEW YORK

BAR TRICKS

A Berkley Book / published by arrangement with
Boldface Publishing

PRINTING HISTORY
Berkley edition / December 1990

ISBN: 0-425-12795-8

A BERKLEY BOOK ® TM 757,375
Berkley Books are published by
The Berkley Publishing Group,
200 Madison Avenue, New York, New York 10016.
The name "Berkley" and the "B" logo
are trademarks belonging to
Berkley Publishing Corporation.

PRINTED IN THE UNITED STATES OF AMERICA

10 9 8 7 6 5 4 3 2 1

I would like to dedicate this book to my wife Marianne and my two children, Christian and Desiree. It is their understanding and grace that allowed me my several years of research in various bars. I would also like to dedicate this to those fearless bartenders and bar patrons whom I have met while doing this research. I owe them many thanks.

Table of Contents

Chapter VI—Mind Blowers 45

Introduction

If you'd like to drink free for the rest of your life, just study this book, study the people who hang out in your local watering holes, make a few friendly wagers for drinks, and there you go...

It goes without saying, though, that you need to use a little common sense. Don't wander into a bar with fourteen large motorcycles parked out front and try to trick a large, surly, inebriated guy dressed in black leather out of a drink.

Also, some of these tricks require time to master, so you don't want to bet the farm on them after one quick reading of the instructions.

But with a little bit of skill, a little practice, and a little appreciation of human nature, you'll be able to win a steady supply of free drinks—all while having fun, entertaining people, and making new friends.

BAR
TRICKS

Chapter I

Simple Straw Fun

1. Martini Glass

The game is played either with toothpicks, matches, stir sticks or straws—all available at any bar.

You form a Martini Glass using four straws and an olive (Diagram 1—shown with matches). Then wager a friend or acquaintance that he cannot remove the olive from the glass by moving only two straws.

The key is shifting the center match over halfway, allowing you to reposition the glass upside down.

Although it looks easy, you will be amazed at the length of time required by some people to figure this one out. The Martini Glass is somewhat of a beginner's trick, but the following four tricks will advance to more difficult feats.

Diagram 1

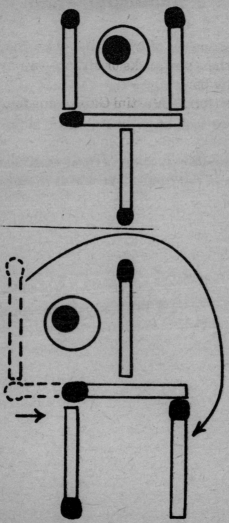

2. Swimming Fish

The Swimming Fish is prepared with eight straws or sticks as shown in Diagram 2. The puzzle is to relocate three straws and have the fish swimming in the opposite direction. This may look easy, but, again, it is far from it.

The solution is to move three matches from the top to the bottom, as shown in the illustration.

Diagram 2

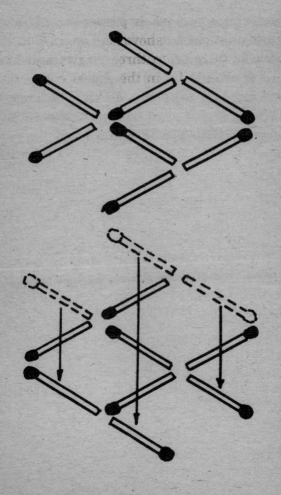

3. Triangles

In this trick you use six straws to make a one-story house with a shed roof on it. You then ask your friend to move three straws to make four identically sized triangles.

This could take him all day, because the secret is that it must be done in three dimensions (as shown in Diagram 3).

Diagram 3

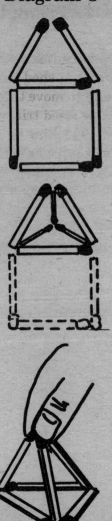

4. Draw Straws Game 1

This game has been around for many years.

You put fifteen straws on the bartop and challenge someone to play. You and your opponent may draw from one to three straws at each turn, and the loser is the player who must pick up the last straw. (See Diagram 4.)

The secret of the game is to leave nine straws on the table for your opponent. After leaving nine straws on the bar, then leave five. Once your opponent is faced with five straws, there is no way for him or her to win!

Diagram 4

START OF GAME
EACH PLAYER MUST TAKE 1, 2, OR 3 MATCHES

AFTER FIRST TWO MOVES, OR SO
LEAVE 9 TO YOUR OPPONENT

AFTER NEXT TWO MOVES, LEAVE 5
TO YOUR OPPONENT

NEXT, IF HE TAKES 1—YOU TAKE 3
      IF HE TAKES 2—YOU TAKE 2
      IF HE TAKES 3—YOU TAKE 1
FINAL MOVE—YOU WIN

5. Draw Straws Game 2

If your opponent figures out how to win at Draw Straws Game 1, issue a challenge for a new game.

Place three groups of straws on the bar—two in one group, three in the next, and four in the final group. Either player may draw first, with the option of drawing either one or any number of straws in any individual group. The loser is the one drawing the last straw.

The secret is to leave the groups in a combination of 3-2-1, 2-2, or 1-1-1. (See Diagram 5.)

Once you have your opponent faced with one of these positions, it is impossible for him to win. The key to Draw Straws Game 2 is to never explain to anyone how it is done.

Diagram 5

START OF GAME
PLAYERS MUST PICK UP ALL OR PART OF ANY GROUP

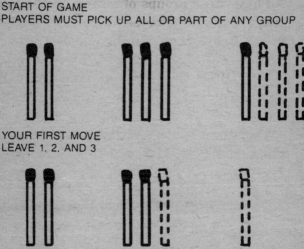

YOUR FIRST MOVE
LEAVE 1, 2, AND 3

IF OPPONENT TAKES ONE FROM GROUP II OR III
LEAVE 2 AND 2 IN GROUP I AND II

IF OPPONENT TAKES ONE FROM GROUP I OR 2 FROM
GROUP II—LEAVE 1 IN EACH GROUP

Chapter II

Bottle Blow Aways

6. Bottle in the Corner

As you travel around the country and spend a little time in bars or saloons, it is always worth a drink to wager someone that you can take a beer bottle and stick it in the corner of the room using no glue or other devices. Very few people have seen this trick, and you can have a lot of success with it. The only requirement is that the room be painted with latex paint.

To suspend the bottle in the corner, put the label side facing you, rub the bottle up and down rapidly against the two facing walls in an almost vibration-like motion. The friction causes the glass to heat the paint to the point that it acts like glue and the bottle will stick to it.

Once you feel the bottle begin to stick, just walk away and the bottle will hang as if magically suspended. Bottles have been known to stay suspended for more than a week.

7. Super Fly

I've never had much luck catching a live fly, but there always seems to be someone hanging around a bar with that talent. If you find yourself in a situation with live flies, and a talented live-fly catcher, you can score big with this trick.

Catch a live fly and keep it submerged in a glass of water until everyone agrees that the fly is dead. Then bet a drink that the fly is *not* dead.

After the bets are down, remove the fly and place it on a small mound of salt you've sprinkled on top of the bar. Urge patience, and then watch as the fly is resurrected and flies away.

I'm no expert in biology, but I assume the salt dries the fly, which only appeared to be dead.

Chapter III

Glass
Gassers

8. Dime into Glass

Ask the bartender to take two highball glasses, submerge them in water so that they fill, place them top to top, and set them in front of you. Your wager is that you can put a dime in the bottom of the glass on the bar without spilling a drop.

This is easily done by taking a bar spoon or other metal object and carefully tapping the top glass on the side until it moves just a bit, just enough to slip the edge of a dime between the two glasses. Then slowly tap the dime until it slides into the bottom glass. *Voila!* You didn't spill a drop.

This works because the surface tension retains the water inside of the two glasses. (See Diagram 6.)

Diagram 6

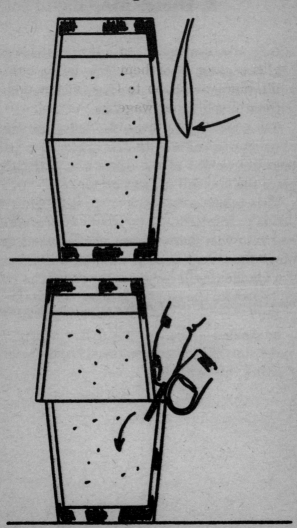

9. Water Straw

After you've won your bet by getting the dime into the glass, make another wager—that you can remove the water from the top glass without touching either glass.

Get a third glass from the bartender and cover the top of it with stir sticks so it will hold the weight of the other two. Carefully place the two full glasses on top.

Then take a soda straw or sip stick, put one end in your mouth and carefully slip the other end into the space where you inserted the dime. Blow very gently, and the water from the top glass will come oozing out of the rim and flow into the empty glass below. (See Diagram 7.)

Be careful—this can get rather messy, so make sure there is a bar towel handy before starting this trick.

Diagram 7

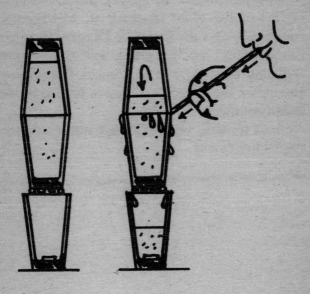

10. Coaster Pickup

Another glass bet is that you can take a glass of water, turn it upside down on the bar, and pick it up without spilling any.

Take a glass about half-full of water (leave at least one inch of air space), place a coaster on top of the glass to cover it, and turn it upside down on the bar. (See Diagram 8.) You can now pick up the glass, and the coaster will stay on to hold in the water. (When you turn over the glass, a vacuum is created to hold the coaster.)

Don't try this with anything but water—it might not work!

Diagram 8

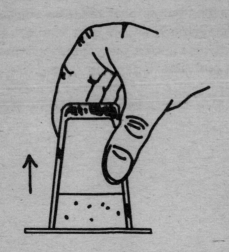

11. Beer and Booze Race

For this trick you need an opponent who is in good humor and can take a joke.

Bet that you can drink two glasses of beer before he can drink one shot of liquor.

There are only two rules:

A. He cannot touch your beer glasses and you cannot touch his shot glass.

B. You get a one-beer headstart, and your opponent can't pick up the shot until you put your first empty beer glass on the bar.

You drink your first beer and turn the glass upside down over your opponent's shot glass. You can then finish the second beer at your leisure while your opponent can only stare at the shot under the untouchable beer glass. (Diagram 9.)

Diagram 9

12. Pennies in a Shot Glass

Ask the bartender to hand you a shot glass filled up to the rim with water, then carefully take a napkin and wipe the top rim to make sure it is dry all the way around.

Take a stack of pennies from your pocket—anywhere from ten to twenty, depending on the size of the shot glass—and wager that you can put all of the pennies into the shot glass without spilling a drop.

Once the bet is made, slowly slide the pennies in from the edge, one at a time, being careful not to get the rim of the glass wet. The surface tension at the top of the shot glass will hold the water inside as you add the pennies. (See Diagram 10.)

This does require some practice, but after the trick is completed, you can see that the water at the top of the glass is bowed out completely, but surface tension holds it in the glass.

Diagram 10

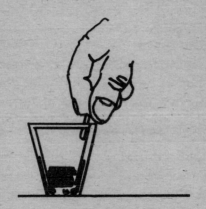

Chapter IV

Dollar
Bill
Bets

13. Bill Through a Lime

Make a wager with anyone who'll take the action that you can take a dollar bill and shove it through a fresh lime. (Any bar should have a fresh lime; you need to find the dollar bill.)

This is worth the price of a drink to watch, so you shouldn't have any sore losers.

Take the dollar bill and begin to roll it up into a conical shape (see Diagram 11). Keep it as tight as you can, starting very small and rolling the bill very tight.

Take the dart-shaped bill and slowly press it into the lime, rotating it in the same direction that you rolled it.

To your own, and everyone's amazement, the dollar will start to penetrate, work through the lime, and slowly bulge out the other side.

This trick takes time and patience, so don't be in a hurry to succeed. You may want to use someone else's dollar bill, since it will be wet and lime flavored at the end of the trick.

Diagram 11

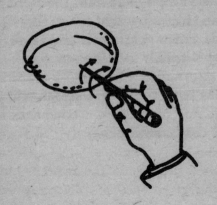

14. Bill into a Straw

This wager is that you can put a dollar bill inside of a normal bar straw.

You need to start with a very flat dollar bill. Starting with the bill lengthwise, keep the ends straight and roll it gently, keeping pressure on with both fingers (see Diagram 12). Be patient and keep the pressure on as you roll the bill smaller and smaller.

Once the bill is down to the approximate size of the straw, hold onto the bill and also hold the straw to warm it up. Start the bill into the straw while continuing to roll it, pushing it gently into the straw.

The gentleman who taught me this trick claims to have rolled up a dollar bill so tight he fit it into a sip stick. I tried that but got the bill only halfway in.

Diagram 12

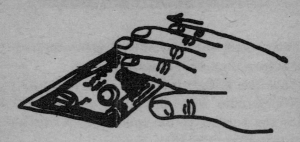

15. Bill Between Two Bottles

Take two very dry beer or soft drink bottles. Make *sure* they are completely dry.

Place the first bottle right side up on the edge of a table, put a dollar bill on top, then place the second bottle upside down on the first (see Diagram 13).

Your wager is that you can remove the dollar bill without touching the beer bottles. Let your friends try first, if they're not willing to take the action right away.

Then show them how it's done. Taking either hand, hold the dollar bill out between your index finger and thumb—straight, fairly tight, but not so tight as to pull the bottles.

Then take the index finger on your other hand and chop it down into the dollar bill as fast as possible, still holding tight with the first hand. The bill should come flying out and leave the bottles standing as if they were never touched.

Practice makes this one perfect.

Diagram 13

Chapter V

Coin
Corkers

16. Coin Under Glass

Since this is a flat-out "trick," only try it with a friendly person.

Take two quarters from your pocket, keeping one hidden in your hand. Place the other quarter in full view on the bar, covering it with a napkin, and then put your drink over it. Wager that you can pick up the quarter without touching the glass or the napkin.

Once you have your bet, play magician and do a lot of hocus-pocus around the drink, uttering some magic words. With the hand that has the quarter in it under the bar, slam the bar with your free hand, then pull out the quarter and put it on the bar.

Chances are your mark will then immediately pick up your glass and napkin to see if the quarter is still there, at which point you are free to pick up the coin without touching the glass or the napkin.

17. Penny Read

A woman bartender pulled this one on me, and I thought I'd throw it in just for fun.

She asked me if I had two pennies. I pulled them out and she said "Let's read those pennies. Do you see any automobiles in these pennies?"

I said no, but she replied, "There are two Lincolns."

She asked if I saw any snakes. I said no, but she said, "There are two copperheads."

"Do you see any fruit?" she asked. When I answered no, she said there were dates on the coins.

Finally she looked me square in the eye and asked, "Do you see any prostitutes with these pennies?"

I said, "Of course not."

She said, "You never will for just two cents!"

18. Penny Spin

Find a very smooth surface—formica works; glass works even better. Take a very new and unworn penny, making sure that on the edge it has no nicks, bends, or crimps. Hold the penny up on its edge, and spin it with your finger as shown in Diagram 14.

Using this method, a penny will come up tails almost every time. The true odds are about nine out of ten, but you can bet on tails coming up every time and keep winning until your opponent realizes that heads won't come up very often.

Again, make sure you have a friendly opponent, especially if you're betting more than spare change.

On a glass top, this trick works something like twenty-five out of twenty-six times, depending on the penny. If your opponent thinks you have a trick penny, let him supply one.

The weight of the penny and the type of spin are what make this trick work. Exclude spins that hit something or do not come to rest on their own.

I have won as much as fifty dollars at one time with this, so don't feel bad—whoever you show it to will be able to win money back from someone else.

Diagram 14

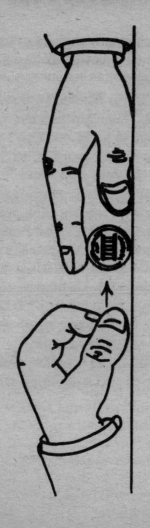

19. Quarter Grab

I learned this trick in Houston, Texas, from a gentleman who had been winning drinks with it for years.

He walked up to me with a quarter in his hand and said, "I can put this quarter in your hand, you hold it palm up, and I can reach down and pick up the quarter faster than you can grab it with your own hand."

That seemed unlikely, since his hand was about eight inches above mine, and I didn't figure my reflexes were so slow I couldn't close my hand before he could grab the coin.

I realized I'd been had when he quickly jabbed my hand with his fingers, causing the quarter to jump from my hand into his. (See Diagram 15.) Even after many attempts, I couldn't hold onto the quarter.

This does take some practice, and you must be fairly sober to pull it off, but it works every time.

Diagram 15

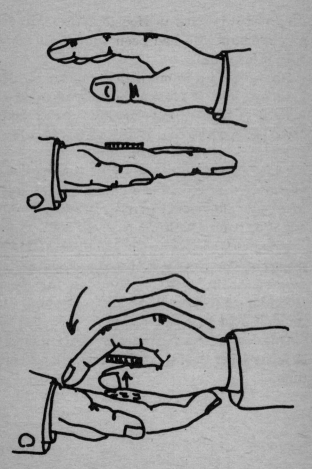

Chapter VI

Mind
Blowers

20. Bar Witch

Take a paper napkin and ask the bartender if you may borrow a fresh lemon or lime. Unfold the napkin and twist the corners up (see Diagram 16) until you make a four-sided tentlike covering for the fruit. Then, shove the lemon or lime underneath the napkin across the bar, making it roll. If you haven't seen this, the gyrations it goes through are almost creature-like and bound to be a lot of fun with bartenders and spectators. Now, go into your kitchen and try the crazy Bar Witch.

Diagram 16

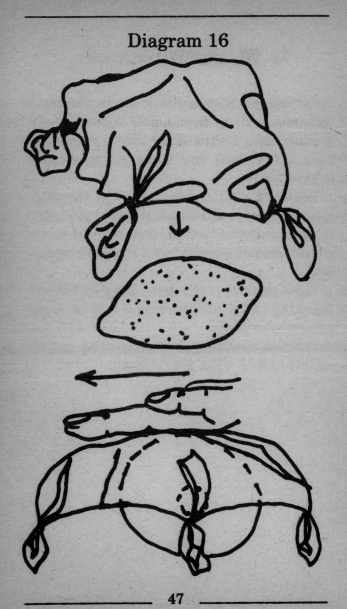

21. Magnetic Cigarette

Start the magic cigarette trick by placing a cigarette in front of you. Roll it gently until it is perfectly round. Keep rolling as you tell your companions that the cigarette is now magnetized.

Then put your finger in front of the cigarette, bend over the bar, and as you pull your finger across the bar the cigarette will follow a short distance behind as if it were magnetized.

What you are really doing is softly breathing on the cigarette, sending it rolling along behind your finger.

Practice breathing on the cigarette so that no one knows what you're doing.

22. The Wizard

With these simple instructions, anyone can be a wizard to impress people and win drinks from them. But to be a wizard takes practice, and requires the help of a second wizard, so share this with a friend who can usually be reached by phone.

Approach someone and ask him to pick a card out of his imagination or from a deck if you have one handy. After he shows or tells everyone the card, you walk to the telephone, dial a number, ask to speak to the wizard, and then say "Mr. Wizard, I have somebody here holding a card." Then hand the phone to your mark, and the wizard will announce the chosen card.

I've had people look all over for bugging devices to find out how the wizard knew the card. If you call long distance, it further mystifies the trick.

Here's how the trick is done:

You and your friend, who are wizards for each other, have a code for the cards.

When you ask to "speak to the Wizard," your wizard slowly starts counting down— Ace, King, Queen, Jack, ten, and so on. When he hits the number, you say, "Mr. Wizard," at which time he knows to start counting down—Spade, Heart, Club, Diamond. When the proper suit is hit you quickly say, "I have a person here holding a card." Now the wizard knows the suit and number. When you hand the phone to your mark, the wizard says in a mysterious voice, "You are holding the Ace of Spades" or whatever the card was.

Once you have the code figured out, you don't need to guess only cards—you can prearrange to guess different things with two simple variables.